Michel

Michelangelo Buonarroti

angelo

Michelangelo Buonarroti

teNeues

Editor in chief:
Paco Asensio

Editor:
Sol Kliczkowski

Original exts:
Llorenç Bonet

Photographs:
© Roger Casas

English translation:
Michael Bunn

German translation:
Inken Wolthaus

French translation:
Clarise Plasteig

Italian translation:
Grazia Suffriti

Graphic design / Layout:
Emma Termes Parera and Soti Mas-Bagà

Published worldwide by teNeues Publishing Group
(except Spain, Portugal and South-America):

teNeues Book Division
Neuer Zollhof 1, 40221 Düsseldorf, Germany
Tel: 0049-(0)211-994597-0
Fax: 0049-(0)211-994597-40

teNeues Publishing Company
16 West 22nd Street, New York, N.Y., 10010, USA
Tel.: 001-212-627-9090
Fax: 001-212-627-9511

teNeues Publishing UK Ltd.
Aldwych House, 71/91 Aldwych
London WC2B 4HN, UK
Tel.: 0044-1892-837-171
Fax: 0044-1892-837-272

teNeues France S.A.R.L.
140, rue de la Croix Nivert
75015 Paris, France
Tel.: 0033-1-5576-6205
Fax: 0033-1-5576-6419

www.teneues.com

Editorial Project:

© 2002 LOFT Publications
Domènech 7-9, 2º 2ª
08012 Barcelona. Spain
Tel.: 0034 932 183 099
Fax: 0034 932 370 060
e-mail: loft@loftpublications.com
www.loftpublications.com

Printed by:
Gráficas Anman. Sabadell, Spain.

September 2002

Die Deutsche Bibliothek – CIP-Einheitsaufnahme
Ein Titeldatensatz für diese Publikation ist bei der Deutschen Bibliothek erhältli

ISBN: 3-8238-5544-1

Capitoline Hill

Palazzo Farnese

Michelangelo Buonarroti (1475–1564) received his training in the neo-Platonic Florence of the late 15th century, an environment which would determine his entire life. By the age of 30, he had already sculptured Pietá (1496) and David (1504), two masterpieces which were highly praised at the time, and which pointed the way for the young artist's future. However, his highly promising potential as a sculptor was not brought to fruition, a consequence of both the socio-political context of the time and the sculptor's personality, and Michelangelo did not complete any of the great sculptural projects of his mature years. The frescoes in the Capella Sistina (Sistine Chapel) were the only work of great importance that he managed to complete, and this in spite of the fact that he always considered himself to be a sculptor first and a painter second.

It was, in fact, the Capella Sistina frescoes that became known as one of the greatest works of art of all time, and one in which all Michelangelo's working methods and personality are brought to the fore. He had sacked all of his assistants and worked alone, for three years, seven days a week, until he had finished the entire work. This gives the impression of an artist with a conscientious approach to his work, and who was not interested in setting up his own workshop, as Raphael and Tiziano did. His method of working, which was slow and meticulous, was interrupted on many occasions by the constant political upheavals of the tumultuous 16th century, problems which were centred around the Lutheran schism in 1517, one of the consequences which – the sacking of Rome in 1527 – would directly affect Michelangelo's situation.

Michelangelo captured the classical legacy of his age and transformed it into an expressive language: the strength that he imparted to his architectural works is comparable to that of his sculptures. He did not see columns and architraves as merely a logical system of supports and weights, but as expressive physical elements which could transform the space and the mass of the building, and would in fact become the main features of his works. Michelangelo was a subtle architect who made use of all the resources he had available to provoke sensations: the spaces and volumes of his works are expressive, and when looking at them the observer becomes overwhelmed by feelings, solemnity, nostalgia, strength and weakness - in short, they are spaces that are impossible to describe in words.

Palazzo Farnese | Dome of Saint Peter's Church in the Vatican | Capitoline Hill

Michelangelo Buonarroti (1475–1564) wurde von dem neu-platonischen Einfluss geprägt, der in Florenz gegen Ende des vierzehnten Jahrhunderts vorherrschte, und der sich sein ganzes Leben lang bemerkbar machen sollte. Vor seinem dreißigsten Lebensjahr hatte er bereits die Pietà (1496) und den David (1504) geschaffen, Meisterwerke, die zu seiner Zeit großen Anklang fanden und die die Zukunft des jungen Meisters begünstigten. Dieses vielversprechende Potential sollte sich jedoch aufgrund der sozialpolitischen Situation jener Zeit und des Charakters des Bildhauers nicht verwirklichen und es gelang Michelangelo nicht, seine großen Projekte später zu realisieren. Die Fresken der Sixtinischen Kapelle sind das einzige bedeutende Werk, das er beenden konnte, obwohl er sich selbst immer eher als Bildhauer denn als Maler gesehen hat.

Gerade beim Entstehen dieses Werkes, das als Krönung der Kunst aller Zeiten betrachtet wird, kommen Charakter und Arbeitsmethoden von Michelangelo zum Durchbruch: Er entließ alle Mitarbeiter und arbeitete drei Jahre lang sieben Tage die Woche, um allein die gesamten Arbeiten zu bewältigen. Hier lernen wir einen Künstler kennen, der sehr gewissenhaft arbeitet und kein Interesse an einer Werkstatt hat, wie zum Beispiel Raffael oder Tizian. Seine langsame

und akribische Arbeit wurde infolge der ständigen politischen Umwälzungen des stürmischen sechzehnten Jahrhunderts häufig unterbrochen. Das Epizentrum dieser Unruhen war das lutheranische Schisma von 1517, von dessen Konsequenzen – hier wäre die Plünderung Roms 1527 zu nennen – Michelangelo direkt betroffen war.

Michelangelo bündelte das klassische Vermächtnis seiner Zeit und verwandelte es in eine ausdrucksvolle Sprache: Die Kraft, die seine architektonischen Arbeiten prägte, ist vergleichbar mit der Kraft seiner Skulpturen. Die Säulen und Architraven bedeuten für ihn nicht die logische Anordnung von Trägern und Gewichten, sondern ausdrucksvolle und plastische Elemente, die den Raum und die Masse des Gebäudes verwandeln, und die die eigentlichen Hauptdarsteller seiner Werke sind.

Michelangelo war ein feinsinniger Architekt, der alle erreichbaren Mittel nutzte, um Sensationen zu schaffen: Die Räume und Volumina Michelangelos sind ausdrucksstark, der Betrachter fühlt sich überwältigt von Gefühlen wie Feierlichkeit, Nostalgie, Kraft und Schwäche... Räume, zu deren Beschreibung die Worte fehlen.

Laurenziana Library

Capilla Medicea

Capilla Sforza

Michel-Ange Buonarroti (1475–1564) suivit sa formation au sein du contexte néoplatonicien de la Florence de la fin du quinzième siècle, ce qui conditionna toute sa vie. A moins de trente ans, il avait déjà sculpté la Pietà (1496) et le David (1504), chefs d'œuvre très applaudis en leur temps et qui laissaient présager du futur de leur jeune auteur. Pourtant tout ce potentiel tant prometteur ne parvint pas à se développer, à cause du contexte socio-politique de la période et du caractère du sculpteur ; ainsi Michel-Ange ne parvint à achever aucun des grands projets sculpturaux de sa maturité. Les fresques de la chapelle Sixtine constituent la seule œuvre d'envergure qu'il put mener à bien, bien qu'il se soit toujours considéré plutôt comme un sculpteur que comme un peintre.

C'est précisément dans la réalisation de cette œuvre, considérée comme l'une des plus importantes de tous les temps que se manifestent clairement le caractère et la méthode de travail de Michel-Ange. En effet, il renvoya tous ses collaborateurs et s'enferma à travailler sept jours par semaine durant trois ans afin de terminer à lui seul la totalité de la tâche. Cela montre un artiste jaloux de son œuvre, loin d'être intéressé par la création d'un

atelier, comme le firent Raffael ou Tiziano. Sa méthode de travail, lente et méticuleuse, fut interrompue à de nombreuses occasions par les problèmes politiques constants d'un seizième siècle tumultueux, avec comme élément central le schisme luthérien de 1517, dont l'une des conséquences : le sac de Rome en 1527 affecta directement la situation de Michel-Ange.

Michel-Ange reçut l'héritage classique de son temps, qu'il convertit en un langage expressif : la force dont il marqua ses travaux architecturaux, est comparable à celle de ses sculptures. Selon lui, les colonnes et les architraves ne sont pas l'ordonnance logique des supports et des poids, mais plutôt, des éléments plastiques expressifs qui transforment l'espace et la masse du bâtiment, les vrais protagonistes de ses œuvres.

Michel-Ange est un architecte subtil qui tire profit de tous les recours qui sont à sa portée pour créer des sensations: ses espaces et ses volumes sont expressifs, et devant eux le spectateur se sent envahi, submergé par les sensations, la solennité, la nostalgie, la force et la faiblesse... des espaces impossibles à décrire avec des mots.

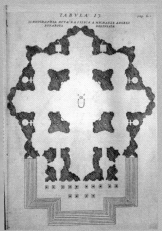

Saint Peter's Church Plan   Perspective of Saint Peter's Church   Perspective of Saint Peter's Church square

Michelangelo Buonarroti (1475–1564) si formò nel contesto neoplatonico della Firenze della fine del XVI° secolo, fatto che condizionò tutta la sua vita. Prima di compiere trenta'nni aveva già scolpito la Pietà (1496) e il David (1504), capolavori assai elogiati nella sua epoca e che preconizzavano il futuro del loro giovane autore. Però questo potenziale così promettente non arrivò a svilupparsi a causa del contesto socio-politico del momento e del carattere dello scultore, e Michelangelo non giunse a terminare nessuno dei grandi progetti scultorei della sua maturità. Gli affreschi della Cappella Sistina costituiscono l'unica opera di grande portata che terminò, nonostante egli continuasse a considerarsi più scultore che pittore.

Proprio l'esecuzione di quest'opera, considerata una delle vette dell'arte di tutti i tempi, mette in luce il carattere ed il metodo di lavoro di Michelangelo: egli licenziò tutti i suoi collaboratori e lavorò sette giorni alla settimana durante tre anni per terminare da solo l'intero lavoro. Questo indica un artista geloso della propria opera e assolutamente disinteressato alla creazione di un laboratorio, come fecero Raffaello o Tiziano. Il suo metodo di lavoro, lento e meticoloso, fu interrotto in diverse occasioni dai costanti problemi politici del tumultuoso XVI° secolo, che ebbe come epicentro lo scisma luterano del 1517, una delle cui conseguenze, il saccheggio di Roma del 1527, danneggiò direttamente la situazione di Michelangelo.

Michelangelo raccolse l'eredità classica dei suoi tempi per trasformarla in linguaggio espressivo: la forza che ha impresso alle sue opere architettoniche è comparabile a quella delle sue sculture. Le colonne e gli architravi non sono per lui una disposizione logica di sostegni e carichi, ma elementi plastico-espressivi che trasformano lo spazio e la massa dell'edificio, i veri protagonisti dell'opera. Michelangelo è un architetto sagace che sfrutta tutte le possibilità alla sua portata per creare sensazioni: gli spazi e i volumi michelangioleschi sono eloquenti, e davanti a loro lo spettatore si sente inondato di sensazioni, solennità, nostalgia, forza, debolezza... spazi impossibili da descrivere in parole.

The Tomb of Pope Julius II

Church of San Pietro in Vincoli, Rome, Italy
1505–1545

The project to build the tomb of Pope Julius II took from 1505 to 1545 to complete. The idea was to build a free-standing construction beneath the dome of the Vatican church which would contain a burial chamber to house the sarcophagus of Pope Julius II. The exterior would consist of a truncated pyramid crowned by another sarcophagus and the figure of the Pope, surrounded by angels. This monument sought to glorify the Renaissance papacy by paying tribute to one of its greatest representatives, Pope Julius II, whose mortal remains are housed within. After 40 years of setbacks and disappointments, the tomb was finally constructed in St. Peter's Church in Vincoli, where it was built onto one of the walls. However, it was a much smaller version and had to be terminated by his disciples; it had also lost all of the heroic nature of the original plans and only the figure of Moses (sculptured in 1513) was used. This figure, which took central position in a group, contrasts with the attempted simplicity of the other images, such as the figures of Lea and Rachel, who personify the active and contemplative Christian life.

Die Bauzeit des Grabmales von Papst Julius II. erstreckte sich von 1505 bis 1545. Ursprünglich sollte unter der Kuppel der vatikanischen Kirche ein freier Bau mit einer Totenkammer errichtet werden, in der der Sarkophag von Julius II. aufbewahrt werden sollte. Außen sollte ein Pyramidenstumpf mit einem weiteren Sarkophag und dem von Engeln umgebenen Papst errichtet werden. Dieses Denkmal – mit den sterblichen Resten Papst Julius II. in seinem Inneren – sollte eine Verherrlichung des Renaissance-Papsttums darstellen, zu dessen bedeutendsten Vetretern Julius II. zählte. Nach vierzig Jahren voller Probleme und Enttäuschungen wurde das Grab schließlich in der Kirche von San Pietro in Vincoli errichtet. Der heroische Ausdruck der Originalpläne ging verloren, als das Grabmal endlich in einer bescheideneren Version von Michelangelos Schülern beendet wurde; lediglich der 1513 fertiggestellte Moses blieb erhalten. Die Figur des Moses steht inmitten einer Gruppe und bildet einen Gegensatz zu der betonten Einfachheit der restlichen Gestalten, wie der Lea und der Rachel zu seinen Seiten, die das aktive und gleichzeitig besinnliche christliche Leben versinnbildlichen.

Le tombeau du Pape Jules II est un projet dont la réalisation s'étend de 1505 à 1545. l'idée initiale consistait à construire un édifice exempt sous la coupole de l'église du Vatican qui aurait contenu une chambre mortuaire où serait déposé le sarcophage de Jules II. L'extérieur devait former une pyramide tronquée couronnée d'un autre sarcophage, et d'une représentation du Pape inanimé et entouré d'anges. Ce monument, renferment les restes du Pape Jules II, devait représenter la glorification de la papauté de la Renaissance, dont Jules II était l'un des représentant les plus important. Après bien des problèmes et des obstacles, c'est quarante ans plus tard que le tombeau fut enfin construit, adossé à l'un des murs de l'église Saint Pierre in Vincoli. D'aspect bien plus modeste et achevé par ses disciples, le tombeau perdit toute la grandeur qui avait été initialement projetée. Ainsi, seul le Moïse, sculpté en 1513 y fut mis en valeur. Cette représentation qui occupe la place centrale d'un ensemble, contraste avec la recherche de simplicité d'autres images, comme celles, à ses côtés, de Lea et Rachel qui personnifient la vie chrétienne active et contemplative.

La tomba di Papa Giulio II è un progetto che si estende dal 1505 al 1545. L'idea iniziale consisteva nell'erigere un edificio isolato, sotto la cupola del basilica vaticana, che contenesse una camera mortuaria dove doveva essere depositato il sarcofago di Giulio II. L'esterno doveva raffigurare una piramide tronca che culminava con un altro sarcofago ed una figura del Papa esanime circondato da angeli. Questo monumento – che ospita le spoglie di Papa Giulio II – aspirava ad essere una glorificazione del sommo pontificato del rinascimento attraverso uno dei suoi rappresentanti più significativi, Papa Giulio II. Dopo quarant'anni e molti problemi e delusioni, alla fine la tomba fu costruita nella Chiesa di San Pietro in Vincoli, addossata ad una delle sue pareti. Molto più modesta e terminata dai suoi discepoli, perse tutto l'eroismo con cui era stata progettata ai suoi inizi e venne utilizzato solo il Mosè, scolpito nel 1513. Questa personaggio, che occupa il posto centrale del gruppo, contrasta con la ricercata semplicità delle altre raffigurazioni, come quelle di Lea e Rachele ai suoi fianchi, che personificano la vita attiva e contemplativa cristiana.

Chapel of Saint Cosme and Saint Damian in Castello Sant'Angelo

Castello Sant'Angelo, Rome, Italy
1513–1516

Castello Sant'Angelo was the fortress to which the Popes would retreat in the event that their lives were in danger, though in the mid-15th century it was converted into the Papal residence. In 1513–1516 Michelangelo designed and created a small façade for the chapel which was dedicated to Saint Cosme and Saint Damian, patron saints of the Medici family. The façade included symbols representing Leo X de' Medici, the Pope who commissioned the project: there are two lion's heads, which are an allusion to his name, while the diamond ring surrounded by feathers that appears on the pediment was the Pope's personal emblem. This is one of the first works in which Michelangelo put his innovative compositional ideas into practice, ideas involving the use of classical architectural features but without adhering to the established rules. The cornices are broken on two planes in order to alternate areas of light and shade, and modillions and other ornamental features were used to give the wall a relief effect; these were techniques which he would later develop during his career as an architect. His sculptural background can be appreciated in the marble used for the surface, which is created to be a volume and not simply a flat plane.

In das Schloss von Sant'Angelo zogen sich die Päpste zurück, wenn sie sich in Lebensgefahr befanden. In der Mitte des fünfzehnten Jahrhunderts wurde es zur päpstlichen Residenz. Zwischen 1513 und 1516 entwarf Michelangelo eine kleine Fassade für die Kapelle der Heiligen Cosme und Damian, der Schutzherren der Medici, die er auch ausführte. Darauf sind die Zeichen von Leo X. de' Medici zu sehen, dem Papst, der das Projekt in Auftrag gab: Der doppelköpfige Löwe spielt auf seinen Namen an, während der federbesetzte Diamantring auf dem Giebel sein persönliches Wahrzeichen ist. Es ist eines der ersten Werke, bei denen Michelangelo seine innovativen künstlerischen Ideen in die Praxis umsetzt und klassische architektonische Elemente verwendet, ohne sich jedoch den geltenden Normen zu unterwerfen. Das Kranzgesims teilt sich in zwei Ebenen, um mit Licht und Schatten zu spielen; er arbeitet auch mit Gesimskonsolen und anderen Zierelementen, um der Mauer Tiefe zu geben. Diese Lösungen lassen bereits die Tendenzen vermuten, denen er während seiner Laufbahn als Architekt folgen wird. Der Marmor, den er nicht als Ebene, sondern als Masse bearbeitet, ist ein Zeugnis seines bildhauerischen Talents.

Le château de Sant'Angelo est la place forte où les papes se retiraient, au cas où leurs vies fussent en danger. A la moitié du quinzième siècle il fut converti en résidence papale. Entre 1513 et 1516 Michel-Ange dessina et exécuta une petite façade pour la chapelle dédiée à Saint Côme et à Saint Damien, patrons des Medici. Dans cette chapelle, on reconnaît les insignes de Léon X de' Medici, lequel fut le Pape commandataire de ce projet ; les deux têtes de lion se référant à son nom, alors que l'anneau de diamants cerclé de plumes qui apparaît sur le fronton était son emblème personnel. Il s'agit d'une des premières œuvres dans lesquelles Michel-Ange mit en pratique ses idées de compositions innovatrices, pour lesquelles il utilisa des éléments architecturaux classiques sans, cependant, se limiter aux normes établies. Les corniches se rompent en deux plans, de manière à alterner des zones de lumière et des zones d'ombre. Il utilisa, de même, des modillons ainsi que d'autres éléments ornementaux pour donner du relief au mur. Ces recours vont déjà dans le sens de ceux qu'il développera tout au long de sa carrière d'architecte. Sa formation de sculpteur se note dans le marbre de la surface qu'il ne traite pas seulement comme une superficie mais comme un volume.

Castel Sant'Angelo è la fortezza nella quale si ritiravano i Papi nel caso che la loro vita corresse pericolo; alla metà del XV° secolo si convertì in residenza papale. Tra il 1513 e il 1516 Michelangelo progettò ed eseguì una facciata per la cappella dedicata ai Santi Cosma e Damiano, patroni dei Medici. Vi appaiono le effigi di Leone X de' Medici, il papa che incaricò il progetto: le due teste di leone alludono al suo nome, mentre l'anello di diamanti circondato di piume che appare nel frontone era il suo emblema personale. Questa è una delle prime opere nelle quali Michelangelo mette in pratica le sue innovative idee compositive, nelle quali utilizza elementi architettonici classici però senza attenersi alle norme stabilite. I cornicioni vengono spezzati in due piani per alternare zone di luce ed ombra, e vengono anche utilizzati modiglioni ed altri elementi ornamentali per dar rilievo al muro, soluzioni che alludono a quelle che svilupperà durante la sua carriera di architetto. La sua formazione scultorea si apprezza nel marmo delle superfici, che tratta come un volume e non semplicemente come un piano.

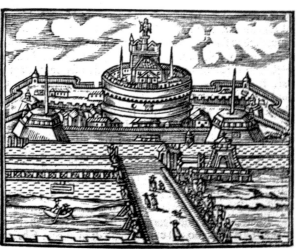

18 Chapel of Saint Cosme and Saint Damian in Castello Sant'Angelo

Laurenziana Library

Church San Pietro in Vincoli,
Roma, Italy
1519

Pope Clement VII donated the Medici book collection to the church of San Lorenzo, and commissioned a space to be designed in which the valuable codices could be conserved and consulted. Michelangelo designed the reading room as an elongated space which would be suitable for study and concentration, and he also took into consideration many other details which would be important from the point of view of the user of the room, such as providing adequate lighting and comfortable desks, which the architect designed himself. The rooms in which the books were stored are located on the same level as the entrance hall, and beneath the reading room. The entrance hall represents a separate world, one which is absolutely expressive. The space is dominated by an enormous three-part stairway which leads up to the reading room. The walls appear to be supporting huge tectonic forces: on the lower level, there are several corbels which are located beneath the columns, as if they were being crushed by their weight, while the columns on the upper level are literally entrapped within the wall. The mixture of proportions makes it impossible for the observer to comprehend the scale, which makes the space totally a-human and produces a strange sensation in the observer.

Papst Klemens VII. stiftete der Kirche von San Lorenzo eine Buchsammlung aus der Zeit der Medici und beauftragte dazu einen Raum zur Aufbewahrung und zum Lesen der kostbaren Handschriften. Michelangelo entwarf einen länglichen Lesesaal, einen idealen Raum zum Lernen und zur Konzentration, und berücksichtigte dabei alle hierzu erforderlichen Einzelheiten: angefangen von der Beleuchtung bis hin zu bequemen Pulten, die er selbst entwarf. Die Nebenräume zur Aufbewahrung der Bücher befinden sich auf der gleichen Ebene wie die Eingangshalle der Bibliothek. Das Eintreten in die eindrucksvolle Vorhalle ist gleichbedeutend mit dem Eintritt in eine andere Welt. Die enorme dreiteilige Treppe zum Lesesaal beherrscht den Raum. Die Mauern scheinen riesige tektonische Kräfte zu tragen: Auf der ersten Ebene treten unter den Säulen Konsolen heraus als ob ihr Gewicht sie zerquetschte, während die Säulen der zweiten Ebene richtiggehend in die Mauer gedrückt werden. Durch die Mischung der Proportionen kann man keinen Maßstab erkennen und dadurch wird der Raum absolut „unmenschlich" und wirkt befremdend auf den Betrachter.

Le Pape Clément VII offrit la collection de livres des Medici à l'église de San Lorenzo, et commanda la création d'un espace pour conserver et consulter ses précieux manuscrits. Michel-Ange conçut la salle de lecture comme un espace en longueur, un lieu adéquat pour étudier et se concentrer, et il tint compte de tous les paramètres concernant l'activité qui allait s'y développer : depuis l'illumination jusqu'au confort des pupitres, eux aussi dessinés par lui. Au même niveau que le vestibule et sous cette salle se trouvent les dépendances où l'on conserve les livres. Le vestibule constitue un monde à part, totalement expressif. L'énorme escalier tripartite qui donne accès à la salle de lecture, domine l'espace. Les murs semblent supporter d'énormes forces tectoniques : au premier niveau des consoles sortent en dessous des colonnes comme si leur propre poids les opprimait, alors que les colonnes du deuxième niveau sont littéralement emprisonnées dans le mur. Le mélange de ces proportions provoque une impossibilité à évaluer une échelle, ce qui rend cet espace « ahumain », puisque n'importe quel spectateur s'y sent étranger.

Papa Clemente VII donò la collezione di libri medicei alla Chiesa di San Lorenzo, ed incaricò uno spazio per la consultazione e la conservazione dei preziosi codici. Michelangelo concepì la sala di lettura come uno spazio allungato, un luogo adeguato allo studio ed alla concentrazione, e tenne in considerazione tutti i parametri necessari all'attività che doveva ospitare: dall'illuminazione alla comodità degli scrittoi, anche questi progettati da lui. Allo stesso livello dell'entrata e al di sotto di questa sala, si trovano gli annessi dove vengono depositati i libri. L'entrata costituisce un mondo a parte, altamente espressivo. L'enorme scala tripartita, che dà accesso alla sala di lettura, ne domina lo spazio. I muri sembrano sopportare enormi forze tettoniche: al primo livello, delle mensole nascono al di sotto delle colonne, come se il loro peso le opprimesse, mentre le colonne del secondo livello vengono letteralmente catturate dentro al muro. Data l'eterogeneità delle proporzioni è impossibile comprenderne la scala, il che rende questo spazio completamente "inumano", e qualsiasi spettatore qui si sente un intruso.

The Palazzo Medici Windows

Palazzo Medici, Florence, Italy
1517

When the Medici family decided to turn their ground floor – which had been used for banking transactions – into a residential section, Michelangelo was commissioned to transform the two access doors into windows without making any alterations to the large arches framing them. The design of these low windows is more complex than their apparent simplicity suggests. Two strong corbels support a small cornice on which the window stands, enclosed by a grille. The transition feature between the cornice and the pediment that crowns the window is a simple rectangular pillar, which is also decorated with a corbel, though one of smaller dimensions. This ornamental feature does not support the pediment, but rather it remains suspended in the air, on the same line as the interior porticoes. Seen as a whole, the work is a rather strange one, both because of the corbels and the imposing rustic arch of the old door, which accentuates the chiaroscuro effect and the dynamism of the structure. This typology, which intermixes the concept of a window with that of a door, has been imitated throughout Europe during the course of the centuries, and is popularly known as a "window on wheels", a reference to its lower corbels.

Als die Medici beschlossen, das Erdgeschoss, in dem bislang die Bankgeschäfte abgewickelt wurden, in Wohnräume umzubauen, erhielt Michelangelo den Auftrag, die beiden Eingangstüren unter Beibehaltung der großen Bögen in Fenster umzugestalten. Für diese tiefen Fenster eine Lösung zu finden war schwieriger als es anfänglich erschien. Zwei mächtige Konsolen tragen ein kleines Kranzgesims, auf dem das mit einem Gitter geschlossene Fenster ruht. Die Verbindung zwischen Kranzgesims und dem das Fenster abschließenden Giebel ist ein einfacher rechteckiger Pfeiler mit einer kleineren Konsole. Dieses ornamentale Element wird nicht von dem Giebel gestützt, sondern hängt in der Luft auf der gleichen Höhe wie der innere Säulenvorbau. Sowohl die Konsolen als auch der beherrschende rustikale Bogen der alten Tür, der den dynamischen Gegensatz von Hell und Dunkel noch betont, erwecken einen befremdlichen Eindruck des Komplexes. Diese Mischung zwischen Tür und Fenster wurde im Laufe der Jahrhunderte in ganz Europa nachgeahmt und ist wegen seiner unteren Konsolen im Volksmund bekannt als Fenster „auf Knien".

Lorsque les Medici décidèrent de convertir la zone du rez-de-chaussée qui avait été destinée aux opérations bancaires locales, Michel-Ange reçut la charge de transformer les deux portes d'accès en fenêtres sans sacrifier les grands arcs qui leur servaient d'encadrement. La réalisation de ces fenêtres basses fut bien plus complexe que ce que laisse croire leur simplicité apparente. Deux consoles imposantes soutiennent une petite corniche, sur laquelle repose la fenêtre, fermée par une grille. L'élément de transition entre la corniche et le fronton qui couronne la fenêtre est un simple pilier rectangulaire, lui aussi décoré d'une console bien qu'elle soit de plus petite taille. Cet élément ornemental ne soutient pas le fronton, il est simplement suspendu en l'air, suivant la même ligne que les portiques intérieurs. Il en résulte un ensemble étrange, tant par ses consoles que par l'imposant arc rustique de l'ancienne porte, qui accentue les clairs-obscurs et le dynamisme. Cette typologie, qui mêle l'idée de la fenêtre avec celle de la porte, a été imitée tout au long des siècles suivants dans toute l'Europe, et on la connaît populairement comme fenêtre « à genoux », en référence à ses consoles inférieures.

Quando i Medici decisero di trasformare la zona del piano terra, che era stata destinata alle operazioni bancarie, in residenza, Michelangelo ricevette l'incarico di trasformare le due porte di accesso in finestre senza che perdessero i grandi archi che le incorniciavano. La soluzione di queste finestre basse è più complessa di quanto si può apprezzare dalla loro apparente semplicità. Due potenti mensole sostengono un piccolo cornicione dove riposa la finestra, chiusa da una grata. L'elemento di transizione tra il cornicione e il frontone che chiude la finestra è un semplice pilastro rettangolare, decorato anch'esso con una mensola, anche se di minori dimensioni. Quest'elemento decorativo non sostiene il frontone, ma resta sospeso in aria, allo stesso livello dei portici interni. L'insieme è strano, sia per le mensole che per l'imponente arco rustico dell'antica porta, che ne accentua i chiaroscuri ed il suo dinamismo. Questa tipologia, che combina l'idea della finestra con quella della porta, è stata imitata nei secoli in tutt'Europa, ed è popolare come finestra "con ginocchia", facendo riferimento alle sue mensole inferiori.

Capella Medici

Church of San Lorenzo, Florence, Italy
1519–1534

In 1519, Pope Leo X de' Medici and his cousin Julius de' Medici commissioned Michelangelo to build a mausoleum for four members of their family in the church of San Lorenzo, in front of Brunelleschi's sacristy. Though the work was left unfinished when the architect moved to Rome in 1534, years later, his assistants added the almost-completed tombs of Julius and Lorenzo, the nephews of Leo X, just as the sculptor had left them. For the articulation of the chapel walls, the architect played with the contrast between the typical grey Florentine stone (called "pietra serena" – serene stone) and white marble, which was used for the tombs. The structure of the tombs helps to achieve a sensation of unity, as there are statues of Julius and Lorenzo standing in niches embedded in the wall, while at their feet stands the sarcophagus, which has a double scroll and is crowned with allegorical images. Light can only enter through the circular window in the dome and several small high windows, and consequently the chapel is bathed in zenithal light that gives the space – one of the most incredible spaces in the entire history of art – a certain serenity.

Im Jahre 1519 beauftragten Papst Leo X. de' Medici und sein Vetter Julius de' Medici Michelangelo mit dem Bau eines Mausoleums für vier Familienmitglieder in der Kirche von San Lorenzo gegenüber der Sakristei von Brunelleschi. Das Werk wurde nicht vollendet, da der Architekt 1534 nach Rom zog. Jahre später fügten seine Gehilfen nach seiner Vorgabe die fast fertigen Grabmäler von Julius und Lorenzo, den Neffen Leos X., hinzu. Die Gestaltung der Mauern der Kapelle spielt mit dem Kontrast zwischen dem typischen grauen florentinischen Stein, dem sogenannten „pietra serena", und dem weißen Marmor, der für die Grabmäler verwendet wurde. Die Struktur der Gräber vermittelt den Eindruck von Einheit, da die Statuen des Julius und des Lorenzo in bogenförmigen Mauernischen stehen, während sich zu ihren Füßen der mit allegorischen Bildern geschmückte Sarkophag erhebt. Das Licht fällt nur von oben durch die Kuppel und durch kleine, hohe Fenster herein und badet die Kapelle in Oberlicht, das diesem Werk, das zu den eindrucksvollsten der Kunstgeschichte gehört, einen Hauch von Heiterkeit verleiht.

En 1519, le Pape Léon X de' Medici et son cousin Jules de' Medici commandèrent à Michel-Ange la construction d'un mausolée pour quatre membres de leur famille, dans l'église de Saint Laurent, en face de la sacristie de Brunelleschi. Le projet resta inachevé lorsqu' en 1534 l'architecte se déplaça à Rome. Bien des années plus tard, ses assistants élevèrent les tombeaux presque achevés de Jules et Laurent, les neveux de Léon X, tels que les avaient laissés le sculpteur. L'articulation des murs de la chapelle joue sur le contraste entre la pierre grise typique florentine, appelée « pietra serena », et le marbre blanc, identique à celui des tombeaux. La structure des caveaux aide à atteindre la sensation d'unité, puisque les statues de Jules et de Laurent sont situées dans des niches directement creusées dans le mur, tandis qu'à leurs pieds s'érige le sarcophage à double volute, couronné par des images allégoriques. La lumière entre uniquement par l'oculus de la coupole et par quelques petites et hautes fenêtres, ce qui fait que la chapelle baigne dans une lueur zénithale, qui donne de la sérénité à cet espace, l'un des plus impressionnants de toute l'histoire de l'art.

Nel 1519 Papa Leone X de' Medici e suo cugino Giulio de' Medici incaricarono a Michelangelo la costruzione di un pantheon per quattro membri della loro famiglia, nella Chiesa di San Lorenzo, di fronte alla sagrestia del Brunelleschi. Il progetto rimase incompiuto per il trasferimento a Roma dell'architetto nel 1534. Anni dopo, i suoi aiutanti montarono le tombe, quasi terminate, di Giulio e Lorenzo, i nipoti di Leone X, così come le aveva lasciate il loro scultore. L'articolazione dei muri della cappella gioca al contrasto tra la tipica pietra grigia fiorentina, la pietra serena, ed il marmo bianco, come quello delle tombe. La struttura delle tombe contribuisce a generare una sensazione di unità, visto che le statue di Giulio e Lorenzo sono situate in nicchia, direttamente nel muro, mentre ai loro piedi si erge il sarcofago, a doppia voluta, culminato da immagini allegorich. La luce entra unicamente dal lanternino della cupola e da delle piccole finestre poste in alto, così che la cappella è bagnata da una luce zenitale che conferisce serenità a questo spazio, uno dei più toccanti di tutta la storia dell'arte.

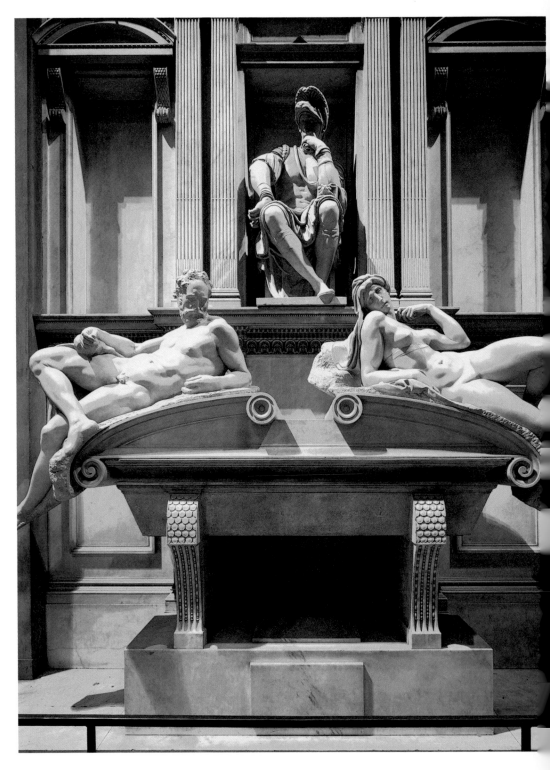

Plan
Grundriss
Niveau
Pianta

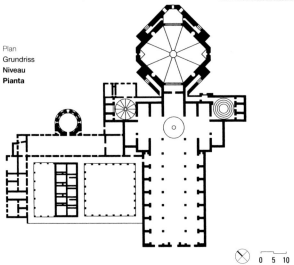

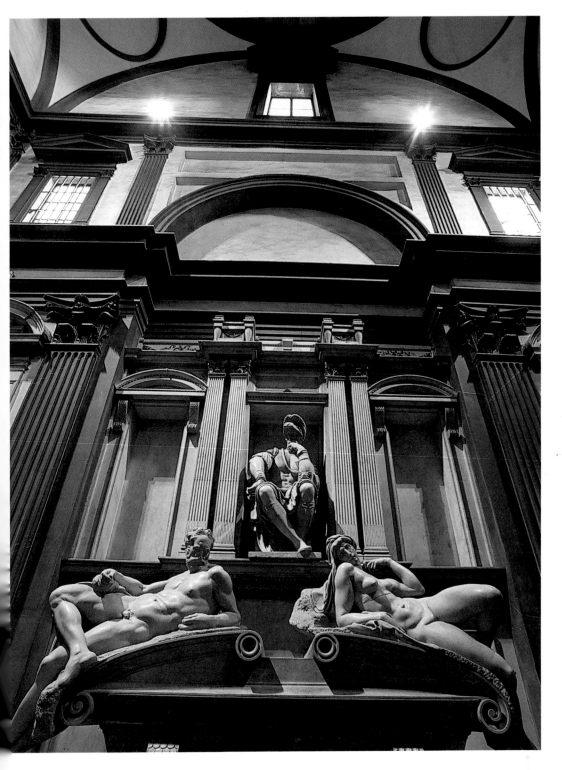

The Capitoline Hill

Piazza del Campidoglio, Rome, Italy
1544–1554

The project to transform the area around the Capitol – that building which had been the focus for politics and religion during the period of classical antiquity – involved in developing an almost impassable space in Palazzo dei Senatori and the Palazzo dei Conservatori. Michelangelo designed a square which is arranged around the statue of Marcus Aurelius on horseback (from the 1st century B.C.), which features a centrifugal flagstone design that homogenizes the trapezoidal space created by the pre-existing buildings. The sculpture, which stands behind the Palazzo dei Senatori (for which Sansovino designed the existing façade in 1615) looks down on the city from the hill, and these two points are communicated by means of a monumental stairway. The Palazzo dei Conservatori (to the right as you come into the square) and the Palazzo dei Senatori (at the end) already existed, and so Michelangelo only gave them new façades. However, the architect designed the Palazzo del Capitol (to the left) as a symmetrical copy of the Palazzo dei Conservatori. Michelangelo created a space which transmits nobility, as well as a certain dramatic touch, owing to the fact that the idealistic sculptor must have felt discontented with the totally corrupt, inefficient government of that time.

Der Umbau des Platzes, auf dem das Kapitol steht – während der klassischen Antike das politische und religiöse Zentrum – bedeutete die Erschließung eines fast unbegehbaren Geländes, auf dem sich der Palazzo dei Senatori und der Palazzo dei Conservatori befanden. Michelangelo entwarf einen Platz um die Reiterstatue des Marc Aurel aus dem 1. Jahrhundert vor Christus herum und hielt sich dabei an das runde Design des Bodenpflasters, das den trapezförmigen, durch die früheren Gebäude bedingten Raum vereinheitlicht. Die Skulptur steht mit dem Rücken zum Palazzo dei Senatori, dessen heutige Fassade 1615 von Sansovino geschaffen wurde. Sie beherrschte die Stadt vom Hügel aus, der mit ihr über eine monumentale Treppe verbunden ist. Der Palazzo dei Conservatori (auf der rechten Seite beim Eintritt auf den Platz) und der Palazzo dei Senatori (im Hintergrund) existierten bereits, so dass Michelangelo lediglich neue Fassaden entwarf. Der Palazzo del Capitol (links) hingegen wurde von dem Architekten als eine symmetrische Kopie des Palazzo dei Conservatori konzipiert. Michelangelo schuf hier ein edles Werk, jedoch mit einem Hauch von Theatralik, was verständlich ist, wenn man bedenkt, dass der idealistische Bildhauer über diese absolut korrupte und zwecklose zivile Institution sicher nicht sehr glücklich war.

Le plan de transformation de la zone dans laquelle se situe le Capitole, centre politique et religieux durant l'Antiquité classique, consista en le réaménagement d'un espace presque impraticable où se trouvaient les palais des Senatori et des Conservatori. Michel-Ange dessina une place qui gravite autour de la statue équestre de Marco Aurelio (datant du premier siècle avant Jésus-Christ), orientée selon le dessin au mouvement centrifuge des dalles du sol, qui homogénéisent l'espace trapézoïdal dû aux bâtiments préexistants. La sculpture, située dos au palais et dont nous devons la façade actuelle à Sansovino, en 1615, domine, depuis la colline, la cité avec laquelle elle communique grâce un escalier monumental. Le palais des conservateurs (situé à main droite lorsque l'on entre dans la place), et le palais des sénateurs (au fond) existaient déjà, ainsi que Michel-Ange ne dessina que de nouvelles façades. Le palais Capitolin (à gauche), quant à lui, fut projeté par l'architecte comme une copie symétrique de celui des conservateurs. Michel-Ange dessina un espace d'où transparaît la noblesse, non sans une certaine touche de théâtralité, puisque ce sculpteur idéaliste devait être insatisfait par une institution civile absolument corrompue et inefficace .

Il progetto di trasformazione della zona dove si trova il Campidoglio, centro politico e religioso durante l'Antichità classica, consisteva nell'urbanizzare uno spazio quasi intransitabile nel quale si trovavano i Palazzi dei Senatori e dei Conservatori. Michelangelo progettò una piazza che gravita attorno alla statua equestre di Marco Aurelio, del I° secolo a.C., retta dal disegno centrifugo delle lastre del suolo, che omogeneizzano lo spazio trapezoidale creato dagli edifici preesistenti. La scultura, situata di spalle al palazzo del Senato la cui facciata attuale, del 1615, si deve al Sansovino, domina la città dall'alto della collina, e comunica con questa grazie ad una monumentale scalinata. Il Palazzo dei Conservatori (a destra entrando nella piazza) ed il Senato (al fondo) esistevano già, così che Michelangelo solo progettò delle nuove facciate. Il Palazzo Capitolino (a sinistra) invece, fu progettato dall'architetto come una copia simmetrica di quello dei Conservatori. Michelangelo progettò uno spazio che trasmette nobiltà ma non è esento di una certa teatralità, giacchè l'idealista scultore doveva essere scontento di un'istituzione civile assolutamente corrotta ed inefficace.

The Capitoline Hill 45

The three palaces not only frame the Capitol square, they also seem to stand back to create different perspectives.

Die drei Paläste bilden nicht nur den Rahmen zu dem Platz des Kapitols, sie erscheinen zurückgestellt, um verschiedene Perspektiven zu erzeugen.

Les trois palaces non seulement encadrent le capitole mais paraîssent être placés pour créer des perspectives différentes.

tre palazzi non solo incorniciano la piazza del Campidoglio, sembra quasi che i pieghino alla ricerca di differenti prospettive.

Palazzo Farnese

Piazza Farnese, Rome, Italy
1546–1549

On the death of Antonio da Sangallo the younger, Pope Pablo III Farnese commissioned Michelangelo to continue the projects that the deceased architect had left unfinished: St. Peter's church in the Vatican and the Palazzo Farnese. Although the architect felt obliged to accept the Papal decision, this commission was not to his liking, as he did not share any affinity with Sangallo's work. Working on this half-constructed palace, Michelangelo attempted to give the façade a little dynamism and to break its monotony by modifying the large central window and the line of windows on the second floor of the interior courtyard. His most personal touch is the upper section of the façade, where the powerful cornice seems to be crushing the entire construction. Michelangelo planned this feature to contrast with arcades on the first floor, but in the end they were not built because they had already been constructed following the designs by Sangallo. What Michelangelo was trying to achieve was the visual inversion of different features: placing the heaviest part at the top of the building, with the arches, and their empty spaces, acting as supports. The cornice on this building has the characteristic expressiveness of all of Michelangelo's work.

Nach dem Tod von Antonio da Sangallo dem Jüngeren beauftragte Papst Paul III. Farnese Michelangelo mit der Weiterführung der von diesem Architekten begonnenen Projekte: des Petersdoms im Vatikan und des Palazzo Farnese. Der Architekt sah sich verpflichtet, die päpstliche Entscheidung anzunehmen, obwohl ihn der Auftrag keineswegs begeisterte, da er keine Beziehung zu Sangallos Werken hatte und außerdem bereits errichtete Strukturen respektieren musste. Bei dem halbfertigen Palast versuchte Michelangelo der Fassade ein wenig Dynamik zu verleihen und deren Monotonie zu unterbrechen, indem er das große Mittelfenster und die Fensterreihe im zweiten Stockwerk der Hofseite veränderte. Sein persönlichster Beitrag ist das mächtige Gesims des Gebäudes, das die gesamte Konstruktion zu erdrücken scheint. Michelangelo hatte vorgesehen, dass diese Elemente einen Kontrast zu den Arkaden des ersten Stockwerks bilden sollten, die aber letztlich nicht gebaut wurden, weil sie bereits in dem Projekt von Sangallo enthalten waren. Der angestrebte Effekt bestand in der visuellen Umkehrung der Elemente: der gewichtigste Teil oben am Gebäude und die Bögen mit ihren Leerräumen als Träger. Das Gesims dieses Gebäudes zeigt die charakteristische Ausdrucksfähigkeit der gesamten Werke Michelangelos.

À la mort d'Antonio da Sangallo le Jeune, le Pape Paul III Farnese demanda à Michel-Ange de continuer les projets initiés par cet autre architecte : l'èglise Saint Pierre et le palais Farnese. Bien que l'architecte se vit obligé à accepter la décision papale, cette commande ne lui fut pas des plus plaisantes, car il n'avait aucune affinité avec Sangallo et, de plus, il lui fallait s'en tenir aux structures déjà dressées. Alors que le palais était à moitié construit, Michel-Ange tenta d'en rompre la monotonie en modifiant la baie vitrée centrale et la rangée de fenêtre du second étage de la cour intérieure. L'apport le plus personnel est le couronnement du bâtiment, où l'imposante corniche semble écraser toute la construction. Michel-Ange avait prévu que cet élément contrasterait avec les arcades du premier étage, mais finalement celles-ci ne furent pas construites, car le premier étage était déjà edifié selon le plan de Sangallo. L'effet recherché consistait en l'inversion visuelle des éléments : la partie la plus pesante en haut du bâtiment, et les arcs, avec leurs espaces vides, ayant fonction de support. La corniche de ce bâtiment conserve l'expressivité caractéristique de toute l'œuvre de Michel-Ange.

Alla morte di Antonio da Sangallo il Giovane, Papa Paolo III Farnese incarica a Michelangelo la continuazione dei progetti iniziati da quest'architetto: San Pietro in Vaticano e palazzo Farnese. Anche se l'architetto si vide obbligato ad accettare la decisione papale, l'incarico non fu di suo gradimento, perché non aveva alcuna affinità col Sangallo ed inoltre il suo intervento doveva limitarsi a delle strutture già costruite. Al palazzo, realizzato per metà, Michelangelo cerca di conferire attraverso la facciata un po' di dinamismo e di romperne la monotonia modificando la finestratura centrale e la linea di finestre del secondo piano del cortile interno. La soluzione più personale è il coronamento dell'edificio, dove il poderoso cornicione sembra che schiacci tutta la costruzione. Michelangelo cercò che quest'elemento contrastasse con le arcate del primo piano, ma alla fine queste non furono costruite perché erano già costruite stando fedeli al progetto del Sangallo. L'effetto ricercato consisteva nell'inversione visiva degli elementi: la porzione più pesante nella parte alta dell'edificio, e gli archi, coi loro spazi vuoti, agendo come sostegni. Il cornicione di quest'edificio mantiene l'espressività caratteristica di tutta l'opera di Michelangelo.

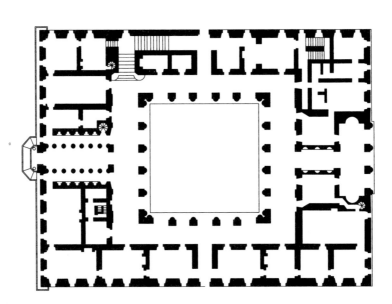

Plan
Grundriss
Niveau
Pianta

0 5 10

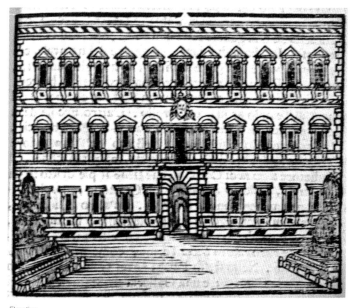

Elevation
Aufriss
Élévation
Prospetto

Saint Peter's Church in the Vatican

Vatican City, Rome, Italy
1547–1564

Michelangelo officially accepted the commission to build the church of Saint Peter in January 1547, and ordered that part of the work done by his predecessor, Antonio da Sangallo be demolished, a decision by which he risked creating enemies among the master builders who were loyal to the deceased architect. Michelangelo's project was totally innovative: the walls were given recesses and projections which alternated with huge Corinthian pilasters that were repeated both in the interior and on the exterior. This dynamism, in which the features remain in a state of tension but none of them stands out from the others, is repeated in the majestic drum, and contrasts with the dome, which is the real hierarchical culminating point of the entire work. Work began on the drum in 1549, and in 1552 a banquet was held to celebrate the completion of the lower cornice. Work continued after the architect's death in 1564, apparently following his instructions, until Giacomo della Porta completed the dome in 1590 and the lantern three years later, though having made a few changes to the maestro's plans.

Michelangelo akzeptierte im Januar 1547 offiziell den Auftrag für die Arbeiten im Petersdom und ordnete den Abriss eines Teiles der Arbeiten seines Vorgängers Antonio da Sangallo an, womit er riskierte, sich die Feindschaft der Anhänger des verstorbenen Architekten zuzuziehen. Michelangelos Projekt bedeutete eine absolute Neuheit: Bei den Mauern wechseln sich sowohl im Innenraum als auch außen zurückgesetzte und vorgesetzte Fassaden mit mächtigen, korinthischen Pfeilern ab. Diese Dynamik mit den unter Spannung stehenden Elementen, von denen jedoch keines über das andere dominiert, wiederholt sich in dem majestätischen Tambour und kontrastiert mit der Kuppel, der wahrhaft hierarchischen Krönung des gesamten Werkes. 1549 begannen die Arbeiten am Tambour und 1552 gab es ein Fest anlässlich der Fertigstellung des unteren Giebels. Die Arbeiten gingen nach dem Tod des Architekten im Jahre 1564 vermutlich nach seinen Vorgaben weiter, bis Giacomo della Porta 1590 die Kuppel und drei Jahre später die Laterne mit einigen Änderungen der Pläne des Meisters fertigstellte.

Michel-Ange accepta officiellement la commande des travaux de l'église Saint Pierre au mois de janvier 1547, et donna l'ordre de démolir en partie l'œuvre de son prédécesseur, Antonio da Sangallo, ce qui lui valut de se faire l'ennemi des maîtres d'œuvres fidèles à l'architecte disparu. Le projet de Michel-Ange était d'une nouveauté absolue : les murs alternent les angles entrants et les saillants avec de puissants pilastres corinthiens qui se répètent tant à l'intérieur qu'à l'extérieur. Ce dynamisme, au sein duquel les éléments sont en tension, sans qu'aucun cependant ne se démarque des autres, se retrouve dans le majestueux tambour, et contraste avec la coupole, qui hiérarchiquement représente le point culminant de toute l'œuvre. Les travaux du tambour commencèrent en 1549, et c'est en 1552 qu'eut lieu le banquet qui célébrait la conclusion de la corniche inférieure. Les travaux continuèrent après la mort de l'architecte 1564, en suivant, semble-t-il, ses indications, jusqu'à ce que Giacomo della Porta achève la coupole en 1590, et la lanterne trois ans plus tard, en y modifiant quelque peu les plans du maître.

Michelangelo accetta ufficialmente l'incarico dei lavori della Chiesa di San Pietro nel gennaio del 1547, ed ordina la demolizione di parte dell'opera del suo predecessore, Antonio da Sangallo, il che gli costò l'inimicizia dei maestri d'opera fedeli all'architetto scomparso. Il progetto di Michelangelo è di un'assoluta novità: i muri alternano rientranze e sporgenze con dei poderosi pilastri corinzi che si ripetono sia all'interno che all'esterno. Questo dinamismo, nel quale gli elementi sono in tensione però nessuno emerge sugli altri, si ripete nel maestoso tamburo, e contrasta con la cupola, vero culmine gerarchico di tutta l'opera. Nel 1549 cominciarono le opere del tamburo, e nel 1552 si festeggiò con un banchetto la conclusione del cornicione inferiore. Le opere continuarono dopo la morte dell'architetto nel 1564, a quanto pare seguendo le sue indicazioni, finchè intervenne Giacomo della Porta il quale terminò la cupola nel 1590, e la lanterna tre anni più tardi, con alcune modifiche rispetto ai progetti del maestro.

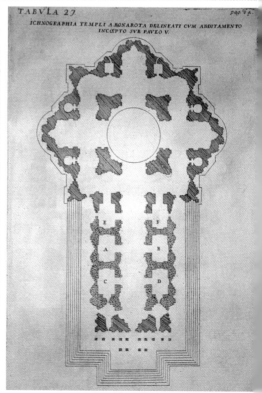

TABVLA 27. pag. 62.

ICHNOGRAPHIA TEMPLI A BONAROTA DELINEATI CVM ADDITAMENTO
INCŒPTO SVB PAVLO V.

PIVS · IIII · PONT · MAX
PORTAM · PIAM
SVBLATA · NOMENTANA · EXSTRVXIT
VIAM · PIAM
AEQVATA · ALTA · SEMITA · DVXIT

PIVS · IX · PONTIFEX · MAXIMVS
ANNO · CHR · MDCCCLXI
STATIONE · PRAESIDIARIORVM · PORTICIBVS · DIAETIS
IN · IPSO · VRBIS · ADITV · A · SOLO · EXSTRVCTIS
PORTAM · NOVO · OPERE · CVLTVQVE · EXORNAVIT
IOSEPHO · FERRARI · ANTIST · VRB · PRAEF · AER

MVSEO STORICO
DEI
BERSAGLIERI

Porta Pia

Piazza Porta Pia, Rome, Italy
1561

In 1651 Pope Pius IV commissioned Michelangelo to remodel the gates of Rome, but the only gate that was actually built was that of Porta Pia, the finishing touches of which were not completed until 1853, and without adhering to Michelangelo's plans. The function of the gate was to control one of the access points into the walled city; it was a revealed brickwork construction in which the stone features stand out, such as this enormous gate, almost three storeys high, which dominates the symmetrical axis of the façade. On each side, two low windows articulate the wall, while a blind window and a small tondo mark the second and third level of the construction. The access gate is divided into two, and the wall is crowned by several graceful scrolls which act as merlons. The gate's pilasters cross the architrave and break the pediment, twisting inside it and turning into modillions. This apparently whimsical feature has been interpreted by critics as being the expression of the limits of all strength. At the age of 70, Michelangelo was more aware than ever that all ascending strength – such as the pilaster – has a purpose, and that is why he created this structure, which turns the entire gate into a spectacular memento mori.

Papst Pius IV. beauftragte 1561 Michelangelo mit dem Umbau der Tore von Rom; leider wurde nur die Porta Pía in Angriff genommen, die erst 1853 ohne Berücksichtigung der Pläne des Meisters beendet wurde. Das riesige, fast dreistöckige Tor, eine Konstruktion aus Sichtziegeln mit hervorstehenden Steinelementen, sollte einen der Zugänge zu der ummauerten Stadt bewachen und ist die symmetrische Achse der Fassade. An beiden Seiten unterbrechen zwei niedrige Fenster die Mauer; Blindfenster markieren den zweiten und den dritten Stock. Das Zugangstor ist zweigeteilt, anmutige Voluten bilden den Abschluss der Mauer und dienen gleichzeitig als Zinnen. Die Pilaster des Tores durchqueren den Architrav und unterbrechen das Giebeldach, in das sie sich hineinzwängen und zu Gesimskonsolen werden. Diese scheinbare Laune wurde von der Kritik als Ausdruck der Grenze aller Stärke verstanden. Michelangelo ist sich mit seinen siebzig Jahren vollkommen darüber im Klaren, dass jede aufsteigende Kraft, wie die der Pilaster, ein Ende findet und aus diesem Grunde schafft er diese Struktur, die das ganze Tor zu einem spektakulären Memento Mori werden lässt.

Le Pape Pie IV ordonna, à Michel-Ange, la rénovation des portes de Rome en 1561, mais seule fut menée à terme celle de la Porta Pia, dont le couronnement n'eut pas lieu jusqu'en 1853, ne suivant plus, d'ailleurs, les plans du maître. Le rôle de la porte était de contrôler l'un des accès à la ville fortifiée, une construction en brique apparente de laquelle ressortent les éléments de pierre, tels que cette énorme porte de presque trois étages de hauteur que domine l'axe de symétrie de la façade. A côté d'elle, deux fenêtres basses articulent le mur, une fenêtre bouchée et un petit tondo marquent le second et le troisième niveaux de la construction. A l'accès, la porte se dédouble, de leur côté le mur est couronné de gracieuses volutes posées comme en créneaux. Les pilastres de la porte traversent l'architrave, rompent le fronton, et y rentrent en se tordant, tout en se transformant en modillons. Ce qui nous apparaît comme un caprice, fut considéré par la critique, comme l'expression de la limite de toute force. A l'âge de soixante-dix ans, Michel-Ange était, plus que jamais, conscient que toute force ascendante, comme celle du pilastre, a une fin, et c'est pour cela qu'il créa cette structure, qui transforme la porte en un spectaculaire « memento mori ».

Papa Pio IV incaricò la ristrutturazione delle porte di Roma a Michelangelo nel 1561, ma si portò a termine solo la porta Pia, il cui compimento non terminò fino al 1853, senza seguire, fra l'altro, i progetti del maestro. La funzione della porta era di controllare uno degli accessi della città murata, una costruzione di mattoni a vista nella quale risaltano gli elementi di pietra, come quest'enorme porta di quasi tre piani che domina l'asse di simmetria della facciata. Ai suoi lati, due finestre basse articolano il muro, ed una finestra cieca ed un piccolo tondo marcano il secondo ed il terzo livello della costruzione. Sull'ingresso la porta si sdoppia, mentre i coronamenti del muro sono delle graziose volute che agiscono come merli. I pilastri a muro della porta attraversano l'architrave e rompono il frontone, attorcigliandosi dentro di lui e trasformandosi in modiglioni. Quest'apparente capriccio è stato interpretato dalla critica come l'espressione del limite di tutte le forze. Michelangelo, a settant'anni, è più cosciente che mai che ogni forza ascendente, come quella del pilastro, ha uno scopo, e perciò crea questa struttura, che trasforma in uno spettacolare memento mori.

PIVS·IIII·PONT·MAX
PORTAM·PIAM
SVBLATA·NOMENTANA·EXSTRV·
VIAM ·PIAM
AEQVATA·ALTA·SEMITA·DVX

Capella Sforza in Santa Maria Maggiore

Via Liberiana, Rome, Italy
1556

Michelangelo designed this work around 1556 for cardinal Ascanio Guido Sforza, and it was built by Tiberio Calcagni. The façade of the church's lateral nave, which was made out of travertine and communicated with the chapel, was destroyed in 1748. The chapel has a central space with a square ground plan covered by Gallonata vaulting (a typical Roman-style vaulting). The main chapel stands on one side, facing the entrance, thus establishing a longitudinal axis. Meanwhile, there are two small chapels on the two lateral sections. The thrusts of the Gallonata vaulting fall toward the wall, in front of which there are several composite columns which advance in a diagonal arrangement towards the chapel, to act as interior buttresses. It is at this point that one can appreciate the tension that exists between mass and space; the columns lead toward the centre, while the space expands towards the lateral chapels, behind the buttresses. Even so, this is not the dynamic tension of his early work, rather it is only a potential, unresolved tension in which the true protagonists are space and the dematerialization of space, subjects to which Michelangelo would return in the paintings and sculptures of his latter period.

Michelangelo entwarf dieses Projekt, dessen Ausführung Tiberio Calcagni übernahm, für Kardinal Ascanio Guido Sforza um 1556. Die Fassade des mit der Kapelle verbundenen Seitenschiffs der Kirche war aus Travertin gefertigt und wurde 1748 zerstört. Die Kapelle umfasst einen zentralen viereckigen Raum, der von einem Balkengewölbe überdeckt ist. Auf einer Seite öffnet sich gegenüber dem Eingang die Hauptkapelle, die eine Längsachse bildet, an beiden Seiten befinden sich zwei kleine Kapellen. Das Balkengewölbe wird von der Mauer abgestützt, vor der sich mächtige Säulen erheben, die sich diagonal zum Kapellenraum vorschieben und als innere Gegenpfeiler fungieren. An dieser Stelle spürt man die Spannung zwischen Masse und Raum: Die Säulen tendieren zum Zentrum, während sich der Raum zu den Seitenkapellen hinter den Gegenpfeilern hin ausdehnt. Dennoch vibriert hier nicht die vitale Spannung seiner ersten Werke, sondern eine rein potentielle, nicht realisierte Spannung, deren wirkliche Bedeutung in der Leere und der Entmaterialisierung des Raumes liegt, Themen, die bei den Bildern und Statuen seiner letzten Epoche immer wieder zum Ausdruck kamen.

Michel-Ange dessina ces plans autour de 1556 pour le compte du cardinal Ascanio Guido Sforza, et ils furent construits par Tiberio Calcagni. La façade de la nef latérale de l'église, réalisée en travertin, et qui communiquait avec la chapelle, fut détruite en 1748. La chapelle présente un espace central de surface carrée recouverte d'une voûte galonnée. Sur l'un des côtés s'ouvre le sanctuaire, en face de l'entrée, qui établit un axe longitudinal : et sur les deux latéraux se trouvent deux petites chapelles. Les poussées de la voûte retombent sur le mur, devant lequel se dressent de puissantes colonnes composites qui s'avancent en diagonale vers l'espace intérieur de la chapelle, afin d'y tenir lieu de contreforts intérieurs. C'est en ce point que l'on peut se rendre compte de la tension entre la masse et l'espace: les colonnes se projettent vers le centre, alors que l'espace s'étend vers les chapelles latérales, derrière les contreforts. Malgré cela, ce n'est pas la tension vitale de ses premières œuvres, mais plutôt une tension seulement potentielle, non résolue, dont les vrais protagonistes sont le vide et la dématérialisation de l'espace, thèmes aussi présents dans les productions picturales et sculpturales de sa dernière période.

Michelangelo elaborò questo progetto intorno al 1556 per il cardinale Ascanio Guido Sforza, e venne realizzato da Tiberio Calcagni. La facciata della navata laterale della chiesa, realizzata in travertino, che comunicava con la cappella, fu distrutta nel 1748. La cappella presenta uno spazio centrale a pianta quadrata coperto da una volta con ovoli. In uno dei lati si apre la cappella maggiore, di fronte all'entrata, che stabilisce un asse longitudinale, e nei due laterali sono situate due piccole cappelle. La spinta della volta con ovoli ricade sul muro, davanti al quale si ergono potenti colonne di ordine composito che avanzano in diagonale verso lo spazio della cappella per agire come contrafforti interni. A questo punto si apprezza una tensione tra la massa e lo spazio: le colonne si proiettano verso il centro, mentre lo spazio si espande verso le cappelle laterali, dietro ai contrafforti. Anche così non è la tensione vitale delle sue prime opere, ma una tensione solo potenziale, non risolta, dove il vero protagonista è il vuoto e la smaterializzazione dello spazio, temi presenti nella produzione pittorica e scultorea dell'ultima tappa della sua carriera.

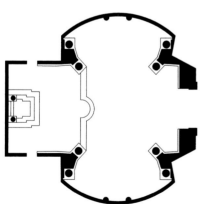

Plan
Grundriss
Niveau
Pianta

 0 1 2

Elevation
Aufriss
Élevation
Prospetto

Santa Maria degli Angeli

Piazza della Repubblica, Rome, Italy
1561–1568

In 1561, Pope Pius IV ceded the Diocletian thermae to the Carthusian order, so that they might build a church with a cloister. Michelangelo created the plans for this remodelling project and work was completed in 1568, four years after his death. In 1749, Vantinelli completely changed the interior wall decoration, thereby destroying the simplicity that Michelangelo had achieved. The main purpose of the work was to conserve the remains of the classical building in a church which would be suitable for use by the Carthusians. The best-conserved part of the old thermae was the Tepidarium, and this was the feature in which Michelangelo was most interested. His design for the Tepidarium hall (which is now the church transept) was highly praised by all of his contemporaries for having succeeded in conserving the eight gigantic columns and the white walls by way of decoration. Thus the great hall retained all the magnificence that was suitable for solemn services, while the everyday rites were held in other parts of the church. In spite of the huge changes which this building has undergone, the church's almost weightless vaulting can still be seen; this was one of the most admired features of the work, and one which reveals the simplicity that Buonarroti always strove for.

Im Jahr 1561 trat Papst Pius IV. die Thermen von Diocleciano an den Kartäuserorden für den Bau einer Kirche und eines Kreuzganges ab. Michelangelo entwarf die Pläne für den Umbau, der 1568, vier Jahre nach seinem Tod, fertiggestellt wurde. 1749 veränderte Vantinelli von Grund auf die Verzierungen der Innenmauern und zerstörte damit die von Michelangelo erreichte Einfachheit. Die ursprüngliche Idee war, die Überreste des klassischen Gebäudes in der Kirche zu erhalten, in der die Kartäuser ihre Gottesdienste abhalten konnten. Michelangelo interessierte sich vor allem für den am besten erhaltenen Teil der alten Thermen, dem Tepidarium. Die Arbeiten im Saal des Tepidariums, das heute das Querschiff der Kirche ist, wurde von allen seinen Zeitgenossen sehr gelobt, weil es ihm gelang, als Dekoration acht riesige Säulen und die weißen Wände zu erhalten. So behielt der große Saal die angemessene Pracht für die feierlichen Zeremonien, während die täglichen Gottesdienste in anderen Räumlichkeiten des Komplexes zelebriert wurden. Trotz der enormen Veränderungen an diesem Gebäude kann man immer noch die fast schwerelosen Gewölbe der Kirche bewundern, Elemente, die die von Buonarroti gesuchte Einfachheit enthüllen.

En 1561 le Pape Pie IV céda les thermes de Dioclétien à l'ordre des chartreux, dans le but qu'ils y édifient une église et un cloître. Michel-Ange projeta les travaux de rénovation, lesquels s'achevèrent en 1568, quatre ans après sa mort. En 1749, Vantinelli modifia complètement la décoration des murs intérieurs, anéantissant de cette manière la simplicité à laquelle avait abouti Michel-Ange. La principale difficulté de ces travaux était de préserver les restes de l'édifice classique dans une église qui s'avérerait commode pour les fonctions des chartreux. La partie la mieux conservée des thermes antiques était le tepidarium, et ce fut celle qui intéressa le plus Michel-Ange. Les travaux dans la salle du tepidarium, à laquelle correspond le transept de l'église actuelle, fut très applaudi par tous ses contemporains, pour être parvenu à maintenir, comme éléments décoratifs, huit colonnes gigantesques et les murs blancs. De cette façon, la grande salle conservait la magnificence requise pour les cérémonies solennelles, tandis que les rites quotidiens seraient célébrés dans d'autres espaces de l'ensemble. Malgré les énormes changement qu'a subi ce bâtiment, on peut encore observer les voûtes presque sans pesanteur de l'église, l'un des éléments les plus admirés et qui mettent en valeur la simplicité recherchée par Buonarroti.

Nel 1561 papa Pio IV cedette le terme di Diocleziano all'ordine dei Certosini perché vi realizzassero una chiesa ed un chiostro. Michelangelo elaborò i progetti della ristrutturazione, e le opere terminarono nel 1568, quattro anni dopo la sua morte. Nel 1749 il Vantinelli modificò completamente la decorazione dei muri interni, cancellando la semplicità raggiunta da Michelangelo. L'impostazione principale dell'opera consisteva nel conservare i resti dell'edificio classico all'interno di una chiesa che risultasse comoda per le funzioni dei certosini. La parte meglio conservata delle antiche terme era il tepidario, e fu quello che più interessò a Michelangelo. L'esecuzione della sala del tepidario, che attualmente è il transetto della chiesa, fu elogiata dai suoi contemporanei, per essere riuscita a conservare come elementi decorativi le otto gigantesche colonne ed i muri bianchi. In questo modo, la grande sala manteneva la grandiosità adeguata alle cerimonie solenni, mentre i riti quotidiani venivano celebrati in altri spazi del complesso. Nonostante gli enormi cambiamenti che ha subito l'edificio, si possono ancora osservare le volte quasi prive di gravità della chiesa, uno degli elementi più ammirati e che rivelano la semplicità ricercata dal Buonarroti.

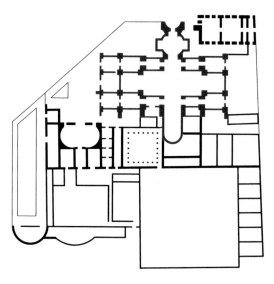

Plan
Grundriss
Niveau
Pianta

 0 10 2

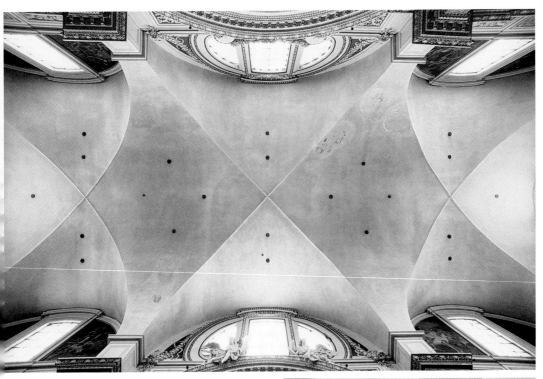

Chronology of Michelangelo's works

1475	Michelangelo is born in Caprese, Italy.
1476–1488	Grows up in Florence, Italy, where he studies grammar and shows a strong inclination towards art.
1488	Joins the Ghirlandaio workshop and is a frequent visitor to the Medici Gardens art school, set up by Lorenzo de' Medici and run by the sculptor Bertoldo.
1489	The student sculptor Torrigiani strikes him in the face and disfigures him, an act that would affect him for the rest of his life.
1492	Sculpts a wooden crucifix (Casa Buonarroti), and later the "Madonna of the Stairway" and the "Battle of the Centaurs" (Santo Spirito church, Caprese, Italy).
1494	Three sculptures for the church of San Domenico in Bologna, Italy.
1495	"Sleeping Cupid" and "Saint John the Baptist" (both lost), Florence, Italy.
1496	Michelangelo makes his first trip to Rome. He sculpts his "Bacchus" and his "Pietá del Vaticano", created for the tomb of the French cardinal Bilhères de Lagraulas, Rome, Italy.
1501–1505	Statues of "Saint Matthew", "Tondo Pitti", "Tondo Taddei", "Bruges Madonna", Florence, Italy. Starts work on what will be his most well-known work - "David".
1504	Sketch for the "Battle of Cascina", Palazzo Vecchio (unfinished), Florence, Italy.
1505	Begins to work on the tomb of Pope Julius II, a project which was completed by his disciples in 1545.
1506	"Tondo Doni", Florence, Italy.
1508–1512	Decorates the vaults of the Capella Sistina, in Saint Peter's Church in the Vatican, Rome, Italy.
1508–1514	Two "Slaves" and "Moses" for the Tomb of Julius II, Rome, Italy. The new Pope, Leo X de' Medici, grants him the title of "Palatine Count".
1513–1516	Designs for Chapel of Saint Cosme and Saint Damian in Castello Sant'Angelo, Rome, Italy.
1517	Design for the Palazzo Medici windows, Florence, Italy.

1519	Designs the façade for the church of San Lorenzo (never completed), the Laurenziana Library and the burial chapel for the Medici family, both in the church of San Lorenzo, Florence, Italy.
1527	Rome is sacked by the troops of Charles V, Pope Julius II locks himself away in the castle of Sant'Angelo. The Republic of Florence is proclaimed.
1529	Michelangelo is named "Procurator General of the fortifications of the Florentine Republic".
1532–1533	Victory, in the Palazzo Vecchio, Florence, Italy.
1534	Moves definitively to Rome, Italy.
1535	The new Pope, Paul III Farnese, commissions him to design the "Day of Judgement" for the Capella Sistina and names him "Supreme architect, sculptor and painter of the Papal palace".
1538	"The Conversion of St. Paul", a fresco for the Capella Paulina in Rome, Italy.
1541	Inauguration of the "Day of Judgement" in the Capella Sistina, Rome, Italy.
1544	Drafts the plans for the Capitoline Hill, Rome, Italy.
1546	Replaces Antonio da Sangallo as architect of the Palazzo Farnese, Rome, Italy.
1547	Replaces Antonio da Sangallo as architect of St. Peter's Church in the Vatican, Rome, Italy.
1553	"Pietá Bandini", which is conserved in the Museo dell'Opera, Florence cathedral, Italy.
1556	Capella Sforza, in the church of Santa Maria Maggiore, Rome, Italy.
1559	Design for the church of San Giovanni dei Fiorentini (never completed).
1561	Builds the Porta Pia, Rome, Italy. Remodels the Diocletian thermae in the church of Santa Maria degli Angeli, Rome.
1564	"Pietá Rondanini".
1564	Dies in Rome, Italy, on 18th February.

Credits

Drawings in the specified pages were taken from the following books:

Bonanni Filippo, *Numismata Summorum Pontificum Templi Vaticani*, Rome, 1696, volume owned by the Library of the University Barcelona, in pages 9, 58, 59 and 60;

Girolamo Franzini, *Le cose maravigliose dell'alma città di Roma*, Venice, 1565, volume owned by the Library of the University of Barcelona, in pages 18, 53 and 71;

Giorgio Vasari, *Vite de'piu eccellenti pittori, scultori e architetti*, Venice, 1828-30. Drawing by C. Rizzardini. Volume owned by the Episcopal Public Library of Barcelona, in the backcover;

Drawings reinterpretated by Loft Publications, 2002.